COME HELL OR
HIGH WATER

COME HELL OR HIGH WATER

Hurricane Katrina and the Color of Disaster

Michael Eric Dyson

A Member of the Perseus Books Group
New York

Published by Basic Civitas,
A Member of the Perseus Books Group

Books published by Basic Civitas are available at special discounts for bulk purchases in the United States by corporations, institutions, and other organizations. For more information, please contact the Special Markets Department at the Perseus Books Group, 11 Cambridge Center, Cambridge, MA 02142, or call (617) 252-5298 or (800) 255-1514, or email special.markets@perseusbooksgroup.com

Design by Jane Raese
Text set in 12-point Apollo

Cataloging-in-Publication data for this book is available from the Library of Congress.
ISBN 0-465-01761-4

06 07 08 09 / 10 9 8 7 6 5 4 3 2 1

To Three Women Who Love and Help Katrina's Survivors

OPRAH WINFREY
Titan of American Media

"I think we all—this country—owe these people an apology. We still don't know how many of our fellow Americans lost their lives in the Katrina catastrophe. . . . They are not refugees. . . . They are survivors and we, the people, will not let them stand alone. They are Americans."

SUSAN L. TAYLOR
Queen of Black America

"Now more than ever, triage among government, business and communities is needed. We must work through our churches and community organizations to secure our people and help them start a new life. This is the proud tradition of African-Americans."

MARCIA L. DYSON
Conscience of the Clergy

"Even though we are scattered, we must be unified. . . . I've heard so many ministers say they're apolitical. Jesus was a political prisoner. The pulpit is the spot where we transformed our situation. . . . We don't want another Katrina to make us love our people."

And to

JOYCELYN MOSES
Strong Survivor of Katrina

"We were in the Convention Center for five days without food, without water, without help. Only way we got food is we had to go in restaurants and stores where people had looted and vandalized to feed ourselves and give ourselves water. . . . We had nowhere to sleep, we had no security, we had no light. We had to survive in the streets. . . . I think that was the worst nightmare I ever had."